The Internet

Davinder Singh Minhas

RISING SUN

RISING SUN
an imprint of
New Dawn Press

NEW DAWN PRESS GROUP
New Dawn Press, Inc., 244 South Randall Rd # 90, Elgin, IL 60123
e-mail: sales@newdawnpress.com
New Dawn Press, 2 Tintern Close, Slough, Berkshire, SL1-2TB, UK
e-mail: ndpuk@newdawnpress.com
        sterlingdis@yahoo.co.uk

New Dawn Press (An Imprint of Sterling Publishers (P) Ltd.)

A-59, Okhla Industrial Area, Phase-II, New Delhi-110020
e-mail: sterlingpublishers@touchtelindia.net
        Ghai@nde.vsnl.net.in

Printed at Sterling Publishers Pvt. Ltd., New Delhi

Contents

Contents

1. Introduction

Internet, also called the **Net**, is an electronic communication device. It is one of the largest networks that links millions or trillions of computers all over the world. You can access this network via communication devices and media such as modems, cables, telephone lines and satellites.

No one knows exactly how many computers are connected to the Internet. It is certain, however, that these numbers are in millions and are increasing at a rapid rate.

The Internet offers many conveniences at your fingertips. You can send messages to others, meet new friends, bank, invest, shop, fill prescriptions, file taxes, take a course, play a game, listen to music, or watch a movie. The advantage of the Internet is that you can use it from a computer anywhere: at home, at work, at school, or at a restaurant.

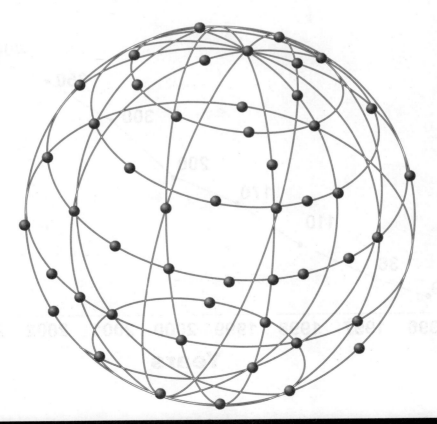

With the help of Internet, you can give a message or even talk to your friend online, no matter where he is, he only needs to have a computer with an Internet connection.

The Internet consists of many local, regional, national and international networks. Although each of these networks on the Internet is owned by a public or private organization, no single organization owns or controls the Internet. Each organization on the Internet is responsible only for maintaining its own network.

At present, more than 400 million people are using Internet for various reasons. The most striking feature of the Internet is that it can be accessed from a computer from anywhere, ie from home, school, restaurant or even from office.

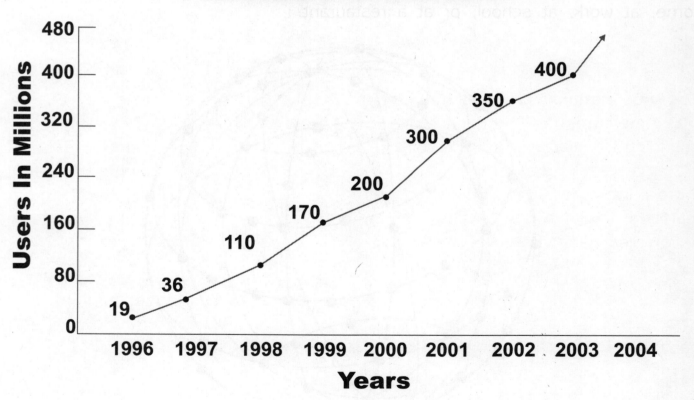

Internet User's Growth

History of the Internet

Let us now go back to the time when many organizations and individuals worked together for years to make the Internet the valuable resource that it is today.

ARPANET

The US Defense Department created a project called **ARPA** or **Advanced Research Projects Agency** in late 1960, which was to work as a network that would allow scientists and military personnel to exchange information in a war scenario without disruption in communications. The network was connected in a way that ensured if one section of the network was damaged, the remaining computers on the network would still be able to communicate with each other and this network was called **ARPANET**. By 1984, ARPANET had more than 1,000 individual computers linked as hosts.

NSFNET

In 1986, **National Science foundation (NSF)** connected its huge network of five supercomputer centers, called **NSFnet,** to ARPANET. NSFnet used the technology developed for ARPANET to allow universities and schools to connect to each other. By 1987, NSFNET could no longer handle the amount of information that was being transferred. The National Science Foundation improved the network to allow more information to transfer. This configuration of complex networks came to be known as the **Internet**.

Most of the people accessing the Internet were scientists and researchers till the late 1980s. In the early 1990s, many companies started to offer access to home users. This allowed anyone with a modem and a computer to access the Internet.

World Wide Web

The World Wide Web (WWW) was created in the early 1990s by the European Laboratory for Particle Physics. The goal of the World Wide Web was to allow researchers to work together on projects and to make project information easily accessible. The first publicly accessible Web site was created in 1991. By the mid 1990s, over 30 million people had access to the Internet. To reach this huge market, most big companies created their own sites on the World Wide Web to sell or provide information about their products. There are now thousands of companies on the Web.

How the Internet Works

On the Internet, data and information are transferred worldwide by the servers and clients which are computers connected to the Internet.

The computer which is responsible for the management of the resources ie programs and data, on a network by providing a centralized storage area is called **server**. The computer which has an access to the contents of the storage area on the server is called a **client**. On the Internet, a client which can access files and services on a number of servers is called a **host computer**. Your computer is a host computer.

The inner structure of Internet resembles the transportation system. In the transportation system, maximum load of traffic is carried out through the highways, which are linked to the major cities. Similarly, on the Internet, there are certain main communication lines which carry the maximum load of the traffic. These lines are collectively called the **Internet Backbone**.

The Internet is a **packet-orientated** network. It means that the data you transfer is divided in packets. So what happens when you transfer data across the Internet's various networks? The networks are linked by special computers, called **Routers**.

A Router checks where your packet (your data) goes and decides in which direction to send it. Of course not every Router is linked with every other Router, they just decide on the direction your data takes. So if the Routers know where the data is going, there must be some kind of an address. Of course, there is an address, namely the **IP (Internet Protocol)**. The data transferred with IP is divided in packets. This is handled by another protocol, the **TCP (Transmission Control Protocol)**.

It was soon discovered that the **IP addresses** (that are, in fact, just numbers) are of course easy to handle for computers, but not for us as humans. So the **Domain Name System** was introduced in **1984**. The domain name is the location of the person's account on the Internet.

Internet Addresses

The Internet uses an addressing system to send data to a computer at a fixed or specific destination, just like the postal system. An IP address ie Internet Protocol address, has its own unique identification attached to a computer or device connected to the Internet. The IP address has four groups of numbers and is separated by a period (.). The number varies between 0 and 255. For instance, the numbers 153.25.15.10 are an IP address. Generally, the first part of the IP address identifies the network and the last portion identifies the specific computer.

It is difficult to remember and use these all-numeric IP addresses. Hence, the Internet favors the use of a text name that represents one or more IP addresses.

The text version of an IP address is the **domain name**. The components of a domain name are separated by periods just like an IP address.

Every domain name contains a **top-level domain (TLD)** abbreviation that identifies the type of organization which is associated with the domain. **Dot com** is the name sometimes used to describe an organization that has a TLD of com.

The **Domain Name System (DNS)** is the system on the Internet that stores the domain names and their corresponding IP addresses. Each time you specify a domain name, an Internet server (called the DNS server) translates the domain name into its associated IP address, so data can route to the correct computer.

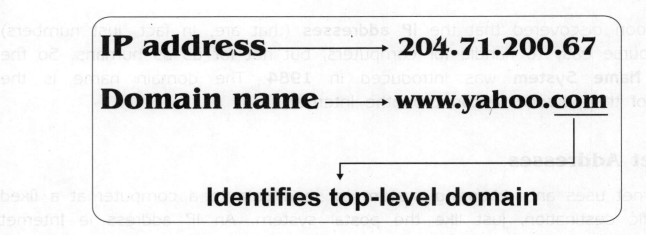

Top-level domain (TLD)

Original TLD	Type of Domain
.com	commercial
.net	gateway or host
.org	non-profit organization
.edu	educational and research
.gov	government
.mil	military agency

Newer TLD	Type of Domain
.biz	a business
.store	goods for sale
.aero	air transport company
.arts	culture/entertainment
.rec	recreation/entertainment
.info	information service
.Name	individuals or families

Advantages of the Internet

The Internet offers many conveniences at your fingertips.

Information

The Internet gives you access to information on any subject imaginable. You can review newspapers, magazines, academic papers, dictionaries, encyclopedias, travel guides, job listings, airline schedules and much more. This makes the Internet a valuable research tool.

Electronic Mail

One of the most popular features of the Internet is the electronic mail (e-mail). You can exchange electronic mails with people around the world. Electronic mail is fast, easy, inexpensive and saves paper.

Entertainment

The Internet also offers different forms of entertainment, such as radio and television broadcasts, videos and music. You can also play interactive games with other people around the world.

Chatting

The chat feature allows you to exchange typed messages with another person on the Internet. A message you send will instantly appear on the other person's computer. You can chat with one person or a group at a time.

Online Shopping

You can order products on the Internet, while sitting at home. You can purchase items such as books, flowers, music CDs, pizza, stocks and used cars.

2. Getting Connected to the Internet

Things Needed To Access the Internet

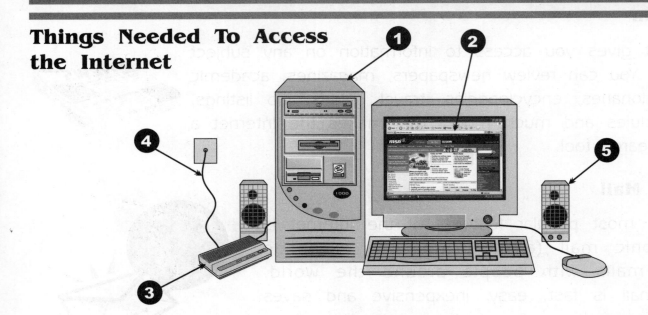

1. Computer

Any computer can be used to get connected to the Internet.

2. Programs

Special programs are used on the Internet. These programs are given free of cost by most service providers.

3. Modem

A modem serves in exchanging information between a computer and the Internet.

4. Telephone Line

All Internet-information travels over the telephone lines.

Or

ISDN Line

Integrated **S**ervices **D**igital **N**etwork is an international telecommunications standard for transmitting voice, video and data over digital lines running at 64 Kbps (*Kilobits per second*). The telephone companies commonly use a 64 Kbps channel for digitized, two-way voice conversations. ISDN service is available in most parts of India.

5. Speakers

Speakers allow us to hear music, voice and other sounds generated by the computer.

6. ISP (Internet Service Provider)

ISP is a company that provides access to the Internet like VSNL, Satyam, Mantraonline, Now, etc.

Modem

Short form of *mo**dulator-dem**odulator*, a modem is a device that enables a computer to transmit data, for example, over telephone or cable lines. Computer information is stored digitally, whereas information transmitted over telephone lines is transmitted in the form of analog waves. A modem converts these two forms.

Types of Modem

External Modem

A modem that is connected on the outside of the computer. An external modem is generally connected to the serial port or USB port. One of the advantages of external modem is that by looking at the display lights on the case, one can quickly check the status of the modem.

Internal Modem

It is the type of modem that is installed inside the computer. Generally, an internal modem installs into a PCI, ISA, AMR, or CNR slot on IBM compatible computer. An internal modem does not provide a series of display lights that inform the user of the changing modem status. The user must rely entirely on the communications program.

Telephone Line

Information is transmitted on the Internet through telephone lines. These telephone lines are the same which are used at your home. When you use modem to access the Internet, you will not be able to use the phone line at the same for making telephone calls. If your telephone and modem share the same line, make sure you turn off the call waiting feature when using your modem, since this feature could disrupt the connection of your modem.

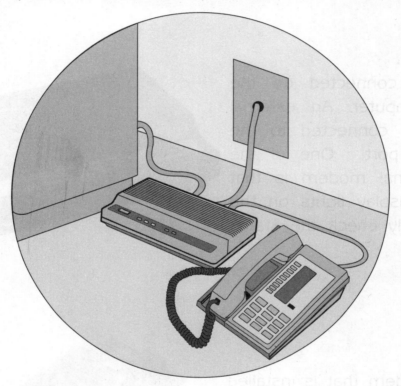

Line Quality

The quality of the phone line can affect the speed at which information travels. For example, a modem with a speed of 56 kbps may not run in that speed if the phone line quality is poor or if some kind of disturbance or noise comes from the telephone line.

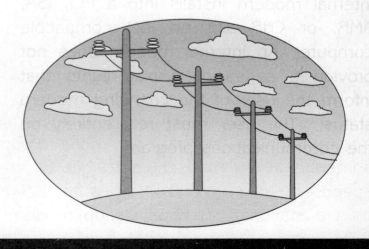

Other Connections

Instead of using the telephone line, you can also use the other high-speed connections to transmit information on the Internet. The importance of high-speed connections are that this connection does not hang up your telephone line while you are on the Internet, so you can make phone calls or use a fax machine while you are connected.

Types of High-Speed Connections

ISDN

It is the abbreviated form of **I**ntegrated **S**ervices **D**igital **N**etwork, an international communications standard for sending voice, video, and data over digital telephone lines. ISDN supports data transfer rates of 64 Kbps (64,000 bits per second).

Cable Modem

A cable modem is designed to operate over cable TV lines. Because the coaxial cable used by cable TV provides much greater bandwidth than telephone lines, a cable modem can be used to achieve extremely fast access to the World Wide Web. This, combined with the fact that millions of homes are already wired for cable TV, has made the cable modem an excellent mode for transferring information for Internet and cable TV companies. Cable modems that offer speeds up to **2 Mbps** are already available in many areas.

DSL

DSL (**D**igital **S**ubscriber **L**ine) is a service that offers a faster Internet connection than a standard dial-up connection. DSL technology uses the existing 2-wire copper telephone wiring to deliver high-speed data services to homes and businesses.

DSL gives 'always-on' Internet access and does not tie up with the phone line. No more busy signals, no more dropped connections, no more waiting for someone in the household to get off the phone. DSL offers users a choice of speeds ranging from 144 Kbps to 1.5 Mbps. This is 2.5x to 25x times faster than a standard 56 Kbps dial-up modem.

Internet Service Providers (ISP)

It is a company that provides access to the Internet for a monthly fee. The service provider gives you a software package, username, password and access phone number. Equipped with a modem, you can then log on to the Internet and browse the World Wide Web and send and receive e-mails. The main ISPs currently available in India are VSNL (Videsh Sanchar Nigam Limited), SatyamOnline, MantraOnline and DishNet, etc.

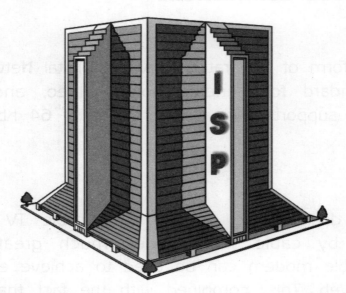

Before going for a connection, one should do a comparative study and then choose the best one available. Some of the things you need to keep in mind while subscribing for a connection are discussed below.

Cost: An Internet service provider can charge you in different ways for the time you spend on the Internet. Many service providers offer a certain number of hours per month for a fixed fee.

Connection Type: The ISP you choose must offer the type of connection you want to use, to access the Internet. For example, if you want to use a high-speed cable modem connection, you will need an ISP that offers cable modem service.

E-mail address: Many ISPs allow you to have multiple e-mail addresses for one Internet account.

3. World Wide Web

The World Wide Web (WWW) is a way of accessing and presenting information in a multimedia-rich form. Graphics, sound, video, animation and formatted text can all be made available via the 'Web'. The information is presented on a page at a time and each page contains highlighted links — called **hyperlinks** — these links could be words, pictures, or graphics. By clicking the **hyperlinks** on web pages, it brings up a new page of related information — this new page also contains clickable links to other pages and so on. A page of text which contains hyperlinks is called **hypertext**.

Why is it called the Web? Perhaps because if you joined up all the links on all the pages on all the computers on all the networks on the Internet, it would just look like one big tangled web.

This method of navigating through pages of information is called **browsing**, or **surfing**. One of the unique aspects of the World Wide Web is that clicking on a highlighted link may take you to a page of information which resides on the same computer, or to a page which is stored on a computer on the other side of the world.

History of WWW

The World Wide Web was developed at the **E**uropean **C**enter for **N**uclear **R**esearch (CERN) in Geneva from a proposal by **Tim Berners-Lee** in 1989. It was created to share research information on nuclear physics. In 1991, the first command line browser was introduced. By the beginning of 1993, CERN introduced its Macintosh browser, and the **N**ational **C**enter for **S**upercomputing **A**pplications (NCSA) in Chicago introduced the X Window version of Mosaic. **Mosaic** was developed by **Marc Andreessen**.

By 1994, there were approximately 500 Web sites, and, by the start of 1995, nearly 10,000. In 1995, more articles were written about the Web than any other subject in the computer field. Today, there are more than a million Web sites with new ones coming online at a staggering rate.

Web Page

Web page is an electronic document on the World Wide Web. A Web page consists of an HTML file in a particular directory on a particular machine (and thus identifiable by a URL). A vast amount of information is provided by these Web pages. The information may include **graphics**, **sound** or even **movies**. Usually a Web page contains links to other Web pages as well.

Web Site

Web site is a collection of Web pages. Most Web sites have a home page as their starting point, which frequently functions as a table of contents for the site. Users need a Web browser and an Internet connection to access to a Web site.

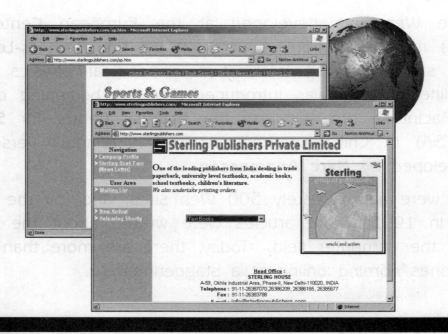

Home Page

It is the first page retrieved when accessing a Web site. It serves as a table of contents to the rest of the pages on the site or to other Web sites. For example, a company's welcome page typically includes the company's logo, a brief description and links to the additional documents available at that site.

URL

URL stands for **U**niform **R**esource **L**ocator, the address that defines the route to a file on the Web. URLs are typed into the browser to access Web pages. The URL contains the protocol prefix, domain name, subdirectory names and file name. Port addresses are generally at defaults and are rarely specified. To get access to a home page on a Web site, only the protocol and domain name are required. For example,

http://www.sterlingpublishers.com

retrieves the home page at Sterling Web site. The **http://** is the Web protocol, and **www.sterlingpublishers.com** is the domain name.

Hyperlink

Hyperlink is a connection between an element in a hypertext document, such as a word, phrase, symbol, or image. The user activates the link by clicking on the linked element, which is usually underlined or in a color different from the rest of the document to indicate that the element is linked. With hyperlinks, one can easily move through a vast amount of information by jumping from one Web page to another. Hyperlinks are indicated in a hypertext document through tags in markup languages such as HTML. These tags are generally not visible to the user.

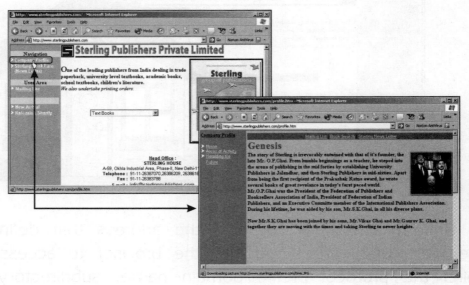

Web Server

It is a computer that provides World Wide Web services on the Internet. It includes the hardware, operating system, Web server software, TCP/IP protocols and the Web site content (Web pages). If the Web server is for internal use, it is known as an intranet server.

The term may refer to just the software that performs this service, which accepts requests from Web browsers to download HTML pages and images.

Every Web server has an IP address and possibly a domain name. For example, if you enter the URL http://www.yahoo.com/ in your browser, this sends a request to the server whose domain name is yahoo.com. The server then sends it to your browser.

Any computer can be turned into a Web server by installing a server software and connecting the machine to the Internet.

Secure Web Page

Some people think that sending important information on Internet is full of risks. They are absolutely wrong, because you can send your information over a secure Web page. It is, in fact, safer than sharing something over a phone with someone close to you.

With the help of Web browsers, security systems that are almost unbreakable are created by secure Web pages. When some information is sent over the net, it may pass through various computers before reaching its destination. If you are not connected to a secure Web page, other people on the Internet may be able to view the information you transfer.

The Web browser will usually display a **lock** or **key** on the screen if it is a secure web page. A secure Web page usually shows **https** rather than **http** at the start of the address.

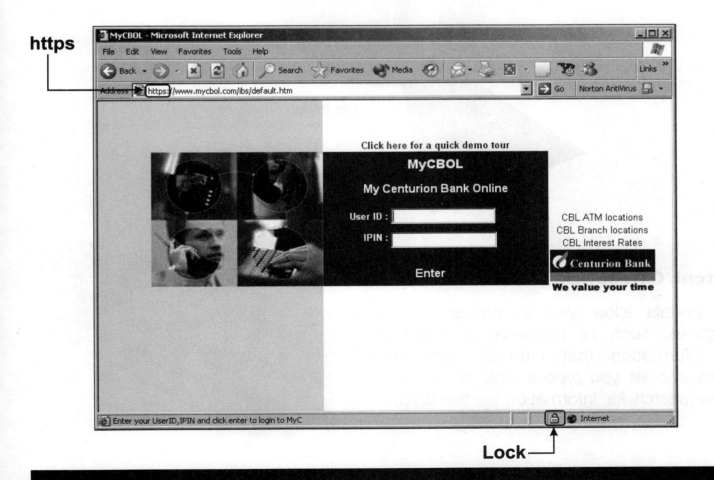

Web Portals

It is a page on the Web that attempts to provide an attractive starting point for Web sessions. Typically included are links to breaking news, weather forecasts, stock quotes, free e-mail service, sports scores, and a subject guide to information available on the Web.

Popular portals include Rediff, Yahoo!, AltaVista, America Online, Dogpile, Euroseek, Excite, GO.com, Google, HotBot, LookSmart, Lycos, Microsoft Network and Netscape Netcenter. The goal of these portals is to be designated as your browser's home page, the first page that displays when you connect to the Internet.

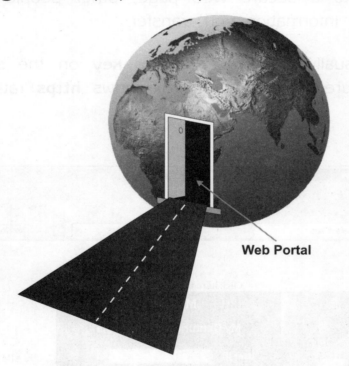

Web Portal

Content Categories

Web portals allow you to browse through categories, such as business or sports, to find information that interests you. Web portals also let you type a word or phrase to quickly search for information on the Web.

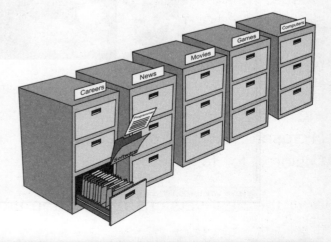

4. Web Browser

A Web browser is a software program that allows to access and view Web pages. Web browser software is built on the concept of **hyperlinks**, which allows users to point and click with a mouse in order to jump from one document to another in whatever order they desire.

Web browsers are of two kinds: text-only browsers and graphical Web browsers. Most Web browsers are also capable of downloading and transferring files, providing access to newsgroups, displaying graphics embedded in the document and playing audio and video files associated with the document.

Browsers have a bookmark feature that lets you store references to your favorite sites. Instead of typing in the URL again to visit the site the next time, you can select one of the bookmarks.

History of the Browser

In January 1993, the first browsers, Viola and Midas, were released for the X - Window system (Unix). At the same time, a Macintosh browser was released as an ALPHA - version.

In February 1993, the first popular graphical World Wide Web browser was **NCSA Mosaic**. It was released for all common platforms (Unix, Windows and Macintosh) in September 1993.

When Marc Andreessen, the mastermind of Mosaic, founded his own company, Mosaic Communications Corp. Now known as Netscape, and released a browser, the Netscape Navigator 1.0. He soon controlled 70% of the browser market. Microsoft saw this gigantic success and soon released a browser, the MS Internet Explorer, for free.

Now the new versions of both the browsers support most of the HTML elements.

Now the more widely used Web browsers for personal computers are Microsoft Internet Explorer and Netscape Navigator. Sometimes, while browsing the Web, when a site says "best viewed by Netscape Navigator" or "best viewed by Internet Explorer", it means that the pages were programmed for that particular browser.

Netscape Navigator

Netscape navigator Web browser is made by Netscape Corporation. Versions of Netscape Navigator are available for Windows, Macintosh and X Windows. It was developed by Marc Andreessen, based on the Mosaic browser. Netscape remains a favorite among many Web users. It provides secure transmission over the Internet, and Netscape server software.

In addition to being a Web browser, this software program also allows Gopher, FTP, and Telnet access, as well as e-mail and newsgroup.

Microsoft Internet Explorer

Microsoft Internet Explorer, also called "IE", is a Web browsing software which was introduced in October 1995 after the Netscape browser had already gained market share. At that time, it supported many of the original Netscape HTML extensions. It is currently the most popular Web browser. Internet Explorer comes with the Windows 98 operating system. It is also available separately from Windows for the Macintosh and UNIX platforms. There are now many versions of IE, and each one strives to offer more goodies than the previous.

Internet Explorer window

When you start Internet Explorer, the Internet Explorer's main browser window opens automatically.

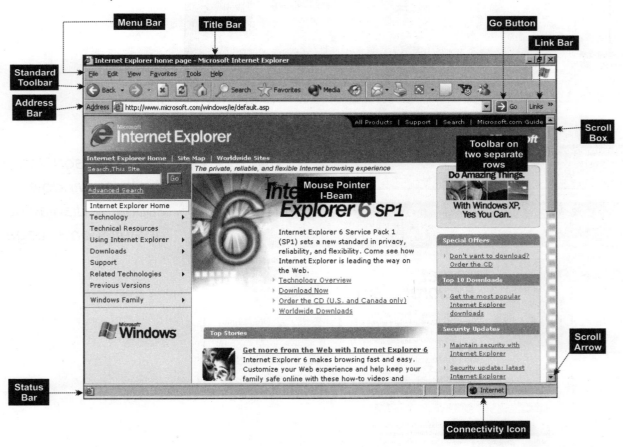

Internet Explorer offers a selection of different toolbars and a Status bar at the foot of the window. The Status bar displays information relating to the transfer of pages and connectivity.

Starting Internet Explorer

To access and view Web pages on the Internet, you can start Internet Explorer.

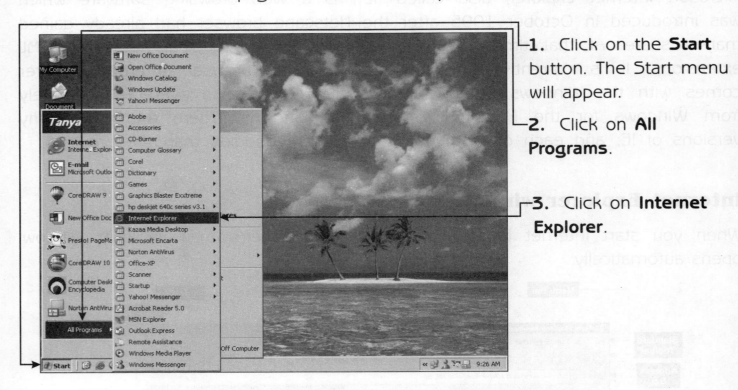

1. Click on the **Start** button. The Start menu will appear.

2. Click on **All Programs**.

3. Click on **Internet Explorer**.

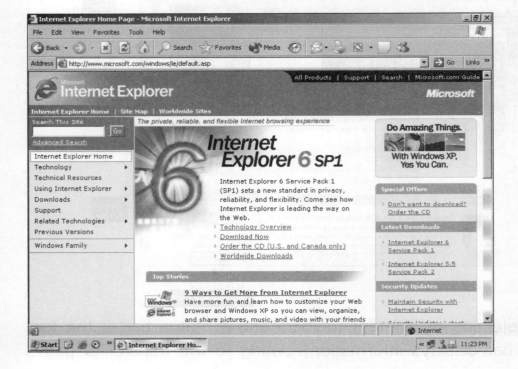

The Microsoft Internet Explorer window appears, displaying your default home page.

Display a Web Page

Any Web site can be opened on the Web using your browser. The only thing one needs to know is the address (URL) of the Web page that one wants to view.

1. To highlight the current Web page address, click on the **Address** box.

2. Type the **address** of the Web page in the **Address** box.

3. Press the **Enter** key on the keyboard.

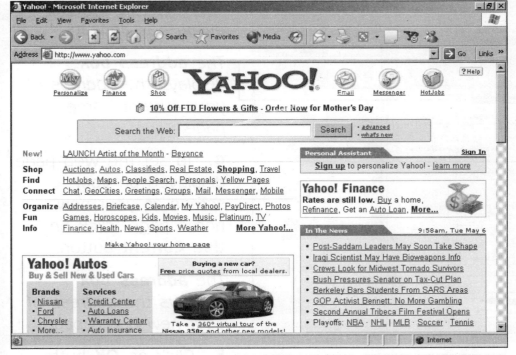

The Web page appears on your screen.

Change Your Home Page

Home page is the first page which appears every time you start Internet Explorer. You can display or even change your home page.

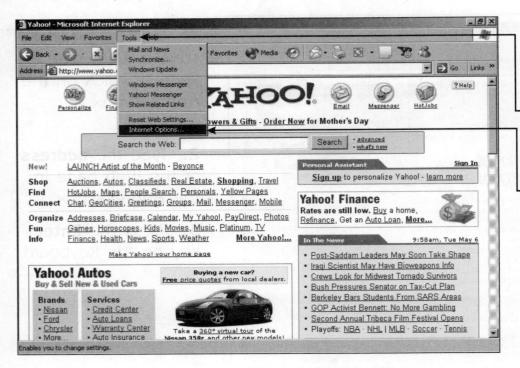

1. Display the Web page you want to set as your home page.

2. Click on **Tools** in the Menu bar. The Tools menu will appear.

3. Click on **Internet Options**.

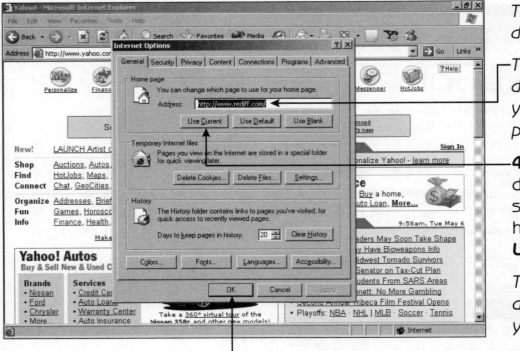

*The **Internet Options** dialog box appears.*

*The **address box** displays the address of your current home page.*

4. To set the Web page displayed on your screen as your new home page, click on **Use Current** button.

*The **address box** displays the address of your new home page.*

5. Click on **OK** button.

Display History List

The Internet Explorer has a **History** list to keep track of the Web pages you have recently visited or redisplay a Web page that you visited previously.

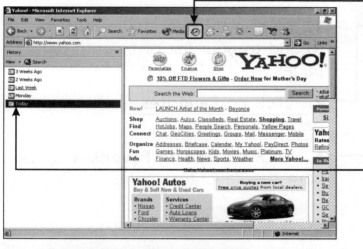

1. Click on the **History** button to display a list of the Web pages you have recently viewed.

*The **History list** appears, displaying a list of the Web pages you have recently viewed.*

2. Click on the **week or day** you viewed the Web page you want to view again.

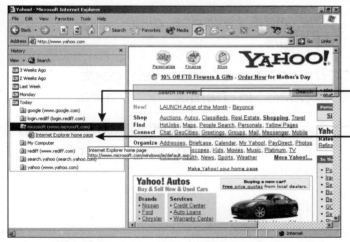

The Web sites folder with files you viewed during the week or day appear.

3. Click on the **Web site of interest.**

The Web pages you viewed at the Web site appear.

4. Click on the **Web page** you want to view.

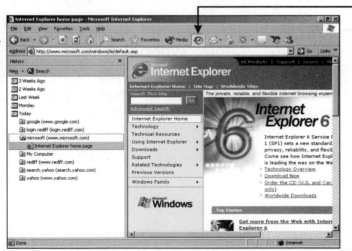

The Web page appears.

5. When you finish using the History list, click on the **History button** again to hide the list.

About Favorites

You can make use of the Favorites feature when you visit a Web site very often. You can display your favorite Web page without writing the Web site address each time you visit a site.

1. Display the Web page you want to add to your list of favorite Web pages.

2. Click on **Favorites** in the menu bar.

3. Click on **Add to Favorites** option from the Favorites menu.

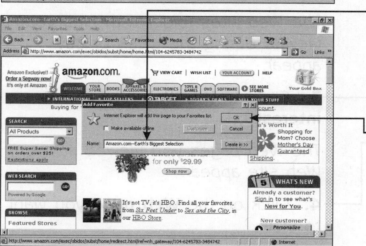

*The **Add Favorite** dialog box appears.*

*The name of the Web page appears in **Name:** box area.*

4. Click on the **OK** button to add the Web page to your list of favorites.

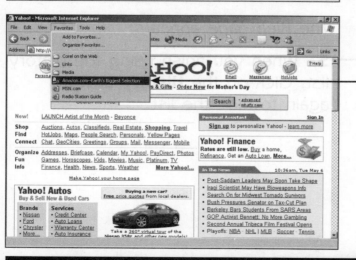

*The Web site address appears in the Favorite menu. Whenever you want to visit that site, simply click on **Favorites** menu and then click on the **site** in that menu.*

5. Newsgroups and FTP

The user conducts discussions on a particular subject in a Newsgroup in an online area. A user sends a message to the newsgroup and other users who read and reply to the message in order to participate in a discussion. A Usenet is the assembly of Internet newsgroups on various topics. Some of them are news, recreation, business, science, and computers.

A **news server** is a that type of computer which stores and distributes newsgroup messages. It is available in many universities, corporations, ISPs and other big departments. For participation in the discussion, one has to enter one's user name and password which is the requirement of some newsgroups. In such newsgroups, only authorised members can participate. For instance, a newsgroup meant for college students may need a user name and password. By this requirement, only students can participate in the discussion.

Newsreaders is a program that is included with most browsers and is used for participation in a newsgroup. Newsgroup is accessed by newsreader in reading a previously sent message, which is called an **article**. One can also post, or add, an article of his own. The newsreader also indicates which articles have been read and which are still left.

The members of Newsgroup always post articles as an answer to another article or as a comment on original articles. These replies may cause the author of the original article, or others, to post additional articles related to the original article.

The original article, along with its subsequent related replies, make a **thread** or **threaded discussion**.

A thread may be short-lived or may last little longer depending upon the nature of the topic and interest taken by the participants.

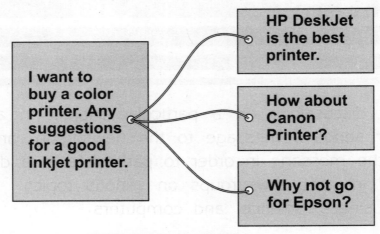

Threaded discussion

In some newsgroups, when you post an article, it is sent to a moderator instead of immediately displaying on the newsgroup. The **moderator** reviews the contents of the article and then posts it, if it is appropriate. Called a **moderated newsgroup,** the moderator decides if the article is relevant to the discussion. The moderator may choose to edit or discard inappropriate articles. For this reason, the contents of a moderated newsgroup is considered as more valuable.

Newsgroup Categories

Newsgroups are divided into sections, or categories. The newsgroups in each category discuss the same general topic.

You can also find newsgroup categories that focus on specific subjects, such as companies or geographic locations. For example, you can find newsgroups that discuss only Microsoft products (example: microsoft.public.win98. Internet) or newsgroups that discuss issues about your city or state (example: abc.delhi).

Category	Description
alt	Alternative
biz	Business
comp	Computer
news	Newsgroups
Rec	Recreation
soc	Social
talk	Talk

Introduction to FTP

FTP stands for **F**ile **T**ransfer **P**rotocol. It is an Internet standard that allows you to upload and download files with other computers on the Internet.

FTP Server

An **FTP server** is a computer that allows users to upload and download files using the FTP.

FTP Sites

An **FTP site** is a collection of files including text, graphics, audio, video, and program files that reside on an FTP server. Some FTP sites limit the file transfers to individuals who have authorized accounts (user names and passwords) on the FTP server. Many FTP sites allow **anonymous FTP,** whereby anyone can transfer the available files. Many program files on anonymous FTP sites are freeware or public domain software. Others are shareware.

Download files

Most FTP sites store huge collections of files that anyone can download, or copy, free of charge. Some FTP sites require you to enter a password before you can access any file. Many people use their Web browsers to download files from FTP sites.

FTP programs

To be able to transfer files to an FTP site, you need to use an FTP program. Many people use an FTP program to transfer Web pages they have created to a Web server. You can find two of the most popular FTP programs at the following Web sites:

WS_FTP Pro (Windows)
www.ipswitch.com/products

Fetch (Macintosh)
www.macorchard.com/ftp.html

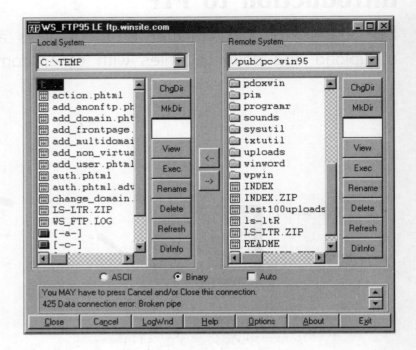

Compressed Files

Large files on FTP sites often are compressed to reduce storage space and downloading time. Before you use a compressed file, you must expand it with a decompression program, such as WinZip. Such programs are usually available for downloading from an FTP site.

Publish Your Web Site

In some cases, you may want to upload a file to an FTP site. For example, if you create a personal Web site, you will like to publish it on a Web server. Many Web servers require you to upload the files using FTP. To upload files from your computer to an FTP site, you use an FTP program. Some ISPs include an FTP program as part of their Internet access service. You can also download FTP programs from the Web.

6. Search Engine and Online Chat

Any single organization cannot control additions, deletions and changes to Web sites. It means that the central menu or catalog of Web site content and addresses do not exist. However, organized directories of Web sites are maintained by many companies, which helps you find information on specific topics.

A software program which is used to locate Web sites, Web pages and Internet files is called **search engine**. It contains massive full-text indexes of Web pages. The quality of search results depends upon the quality of indexes and how the engines use the information. Back-of-the-book indexes are quite familiar to all of us which are alphabetized lists of the important words in the book, and the pages where they appear. Search engine indexes are like back-of-the-book indexes but it is more complex.

A Web page's name that lists as the result of a search is called a **hit**. For example, if you want an information of Gurudwara Bangla Sahib, which is situated in Delhi, you could enter 'Gurudwara Bangla Sahib' as your search text. The search engine would return a list of Web page names that contain the phrase Gurudwara Bangla Sahib. You can then click on an appropriate link in the list to display the associated Web site or Web page. When you enter the search text that contains multiple keywords, the search engine usually locates sites that contain all of the words.

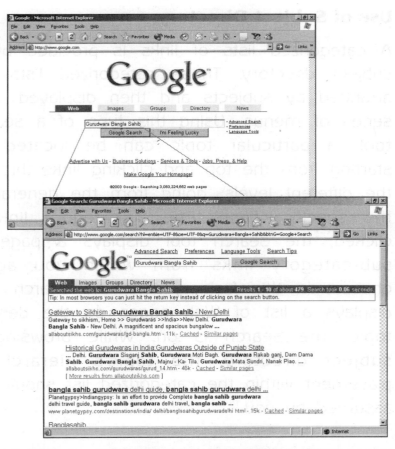

What Are Spiders?

Many search engines use a program called **spider** to display a list of all Web pages which contain the word or phrase you entered. A **spider** also called a **crawler**, is a program which reads pages on Web sites in order to create a catalog or index of hits.

The popular search tools are subject directories and search engines. A **subject directory** is used by clicking through its collection of categories and sub-categories until you reach the information you want. A **search engine** is used to search for a keyword. The following sections describe how to use a subject directory and a search engine.

Use of Subject Directory

A categorized lists of links is provided by a subject directory. These categorized lists are arranged by subjects and then displayed in a series of menus. Using this type of a search tool, a particular topic can be located by starting from the top and clicking links through the different levels, going from the general to the specific. Each time a category link is clicked, the search tool displays a page of sub-category links from which you again choose. In this fashion, until the search tool displays a list of Web pages on the desired topic, the search is on. While browsing a subject directory, the topic's hierarchical placement within the categorized list should be assumed by you.

Web Search Categories

- Astrology
- Sports
- Business
- Jobs
- Movies
- Books

Search Results

1. Cricket
2. Football
3. Table Tannis
4. Baseball
5. Basketball

Uses of Search Engines

One should enter text or keywords (single word, words, or phrase) while looking for a subject, rather than clicking through menus of links. Search engines often respond with results that include thousands of links to Web pages, many of which have little or no bearing on the information you are seeking.

The following are the list of search engines in which you can search for any information.

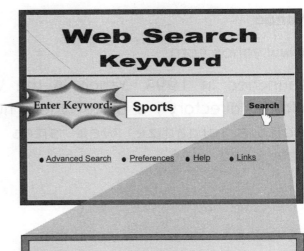

MAJOR SEARCH ENGINES

Google

www.google.com

Google has a well-deserved reputation as one of the top search engines. Google was a Stanford University project by students Larry Page and Sergey Brin originally called BackRub. By 1998, the name had been changed to Google, and the project jumped off the campus and became a company named Google.

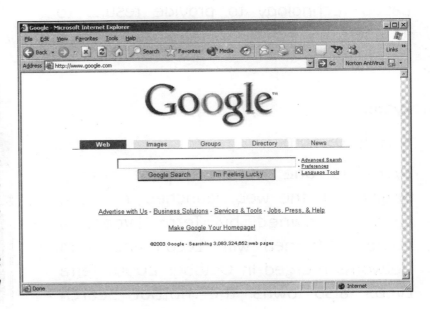

Yahoo

www.yahoo.com

Launched in 1994, Yahoo is the Web's oldest 'directory', a place where human editors organize Web sites into categories.

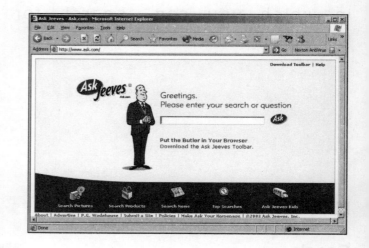

Ask Jeeves

www.askjeeves.com

Ask Jeeves initially gained fame in 1998 and 1999 as being the 'natural language' search engine that lets you search by asking questions and responded with what seemed to be the right answer to everything. Today, Ask Jeeves instead depends on crawler-based technology to provide results to its users.

Lycos

www.lycos.com

Lycos is one of the oldest search engines on the web, launched in 1994. Lycos is owned by Terra Lycos, a company formed with Lycos and Terra Networks merged in October 2000. Terra Lycos also owns the HotBot search engine.

LookSmart (www.looksmart.com)

LookSmart is a human-compiled directory of Web sites. The company operated its own Web site, but this really wasn't intended for the public to use. When LookSmart launched independently in October 1996, it was backed by Reader's Digest for about a year, and then company executives bought back control of the service.

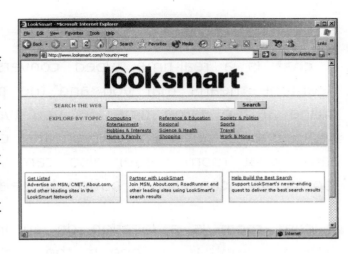

AltaVista (www.altavista.com)

AltaVista is the oldest crawler-based search engine on the web. It opened in December 1995 and for several years it was the 'Google' of its day, in terms of providing relevant results and having a loyal group of users that loved the service. AltaVista was originally owned by Digital, then taken over by Compaq, when that company had purchased Digital in 1998.

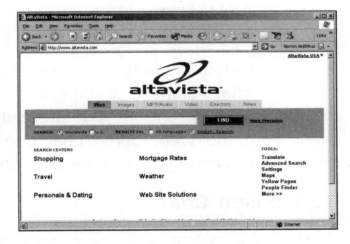

Alltheweb.com (www.alltheweb.com)

It is an excellent crawler-based search engine. If you tried Google and didn't find it, Alltheweb should probably be next on your list. Indeed, it's a first choice search engine, for some. In addition to web page results, Alltheweb.com provides the ability to search for news stories, pictures, video clips, MP3s and FTP files. Until recently, Alltheweb.com was owned by a company called FAST. However, the search engine was purchased by search provider Overture in late April 2003.

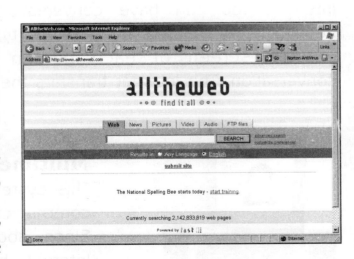

Introduction to Chat

A **chat** is a real-time typed conversation which takes place on a computer. Real-time means that you and the people with whom you are conversing are online at the same time. As you type on your keyboard, a line of characters and symbols get displayed on the computer screen. Others connected to the same chat room server also can see what you have typed. In some chat rooms, you can click a button to see a profile of someone in the chat room.

A **chat room** is a location on an Internet server that permits users to chat with one another. Anyone in the chat room can participate in the conversation, which usually is confined to a particular topic. Some chat rooms support **voice chats** and **video chats,** where you hear or see others and they can hear or see you as you chat.

To start a chat session, you have to connect to a chat server through a chat client. A **chat client** is a program on your computer. Modern browsers usually include a chat client. If your browser does not have, you can download a chat client from the Web. Some chat clients are text-based. Others support graphical chats also, where you can assume the appearance of a fictitious character.

Text-based Chat

This is the oldest and most popular type of chat on the Internet. You can have conversations with one or more people. While chatting, the text you type immediately appears on the screen of each person participating in the conversation. The Internet transfers the text within no time.

Hari: How are you
Rohan: I am fine
Hari: Whats going on
Rohan: Nothing just planning to go for a movie.
Hari: Wow! Thats great which movie are you planning?

Multimedia

This system allows to have voice conversations and communicate through live video over the Internet. Since sound and video transfer slowly over the Internet, hence to use multimedia chat you need a high-speed connection.